Mental Toughness Bundle

Self Discipline
Mental Toughness
&
Meditation For Beginners

By Martin Brandt

Self-Discipline

Mental Toughness

A Guide to Developing Your Grit and Increasing Your Productivity

Contents

Introduction

Congratulations on downloading your personal copy of *Self-Discipline and Mental Toughness: A Guide to Developing Your Grit and Increasing Your Productivity.* Thank you for doing so.

Self-discipline is a useful, important life skill necessary for successful people. Regardless of the area of life you're setting goals in, this skill will be essential. Although most people already know that it's important, there aren't many who actually take proactive steps to build and strengthen it in themselves.

The Misconception About Self-Discipline

There's a common belief about self-discipline being restrictive, tough, harsh, or limiting, but this is far from true. Self-discipline is about inner strength, knowing yourself, and having control. This valuable trait will allow you to follow through on your decisions, stick to your path, and accomplish amazing feats in life.

What Can This Trait Give You?

You will overcome laziness and procrastination, beat addictions, and radiate a strong sense of will. This book will give you the tools you need to build up a powerful sense of self-discipline, the fuel for your greatest desires. As you can see, you have nothing to lose other than some bad habits. So, if you're ready to change your life for the better, let's get to it. Thank you for choosing this book!

Chapter 1: Success, Motivation, and Choices

Success is something all of us crave, whether it's an ideal of how we want to look, how much money we'll earn, or even the type of family we'll eventually have. The idea of success almost seems, to many of us, like an elusive secret. We glorify the concept, place those who have success on a pedestal, and separate ourselves from it. But the truth is, success isn't a secret. If this is true, what is success? It's a *process*.

The Success Process

Success is not something you suddenly achieve one day; it's an attitude, a way of thinking, and a path to living. The subject that you want to gain self-discipline in will be highly personal for you, but there are some general guidelines that can help you along the way. How can you begin the process of success?

- **Define What Success Means to You:** Take some time to really think about this. What is the most important thing in the world to you? Who do you want to reach with your message? What does the ultimate vision of success look like for you? How will you know when you've gotten there? As soon as you have defined success for yourself, you'll be able to get on the path towards it.

- **Know Your Vision is Possible:** You won't be able to work towards your goal if you don't already believe in your heart it can happen for you. Once you've figured out what you desire, seek out other people who have already achieved this goal (either in person, in books, or online). This will inspire you and give you proof that your goal is possible!

- **Act No Matter What:** If you're going to wait around for the perfect time to act, you'll be waiting forever. You cannot depend on always feeling motivated to do something, even when it's something you deeply care about. Force yourself to take action, even on days that you're feeling lazy, and it will seriously pay off.

- **Try to Help Others:** Humans are social beings. We need connection. Providing and giving value to those around you will help you build stronger social ties that you can fall back on during hard times. Helping other people can also inspire us to stay on our personal path toward success. Instead of asking what you can get from any social interaction you're having, ask yourself what you can give. Success is not something selfish, but something only meaningful when it's shared.

The Truth About Motivation

How does motivation work? Oftentimes, this word brings thoughts of bonuses at work, material gains, or extra vacation. But the reality is, motivation is something more elusive than that. It's highly personal and, at times, not even reliable.

Deep, Intrinsic Motivation

If you aren't truly motivated to do a task, intrinsically (meaning you love doing it for its own sake), you probably won't do it. If you're only motivated by external awards, you likely won't stick to your goal.

Take the example of wanting to lose weight. Telling yourself you'll look much better may work for the first week in terms of getting you to the gym, but eventually, you will probably stop going. Reminding yourself that you want a longer life and that you deserve to feel great from the inside out, on the other hand, can be an intrinsic, meaningful source of motivation.

When and Why Motivation Doesn't Work

Sometimes, motivation just isn't effective. No matter how good our intentions are, all it takes is a different mood to slip up on our goals. Motivation can be a fleeting, changing state. This is why you can set your alarm at night, feeling motivated to arise at 6 in the morning and have a super productive day, only to groan and hit snooze when it goes off. For this reason, self-discipline is a far more reliable system than motivation.

You Have a Choice in Life

We have all been around people who seem to lose their minds when something stressful happens, completely shutting down and giving up. They act as though their states of being are out of their control, essentially forfeiting their own choice in the matter. But the truth is that though we can't always control stressful events in life, we can control how we react to them.

An event outside of you can only cause you to stress out if you make the choice to do so. I understand that when you're in the midst of a chaotic situation, your reaction feels like anything but a choice. But the fact is that stress is something we all go through in life. What differs is how we handle it and the best way to control how we handle it is through self-discipline. If you don't have a strong enough desire to learn how to handle stress in the right way, you won't do it. It's a decision.

Stress is constantly around us, but it doesn't become a part of you until you accept and internalize it. Everyone engages in stressed-out behavior every so often, but it doesn't have to be a habit. Here are the steps to control your reactions:

- **Notice them:** When an event pops up that makes you veer off course (whether it's giving up on your goal of losing weight and deciding to eat donuts or procrastinating on that test you're supposed to be studying for), notice it. What are the triggers that throw you off?

- **Record them:** The next step will be to write these triggers down along with the results that came from them. Now, these may not be nice to look at, but a truly self-disciplined person isn't afraid to view their faults. Only when you know what they are can you control and improve them.

- **Tiny Steps:** Now that you're fully aware of your weaknesses, it's time to make small changes toward shifting them. If you know, for example, that walking through the mall and smelling popcorn triggers you to want to give up on your healthy eating plan, stay away from the mall. If you tend to get angry whenever a certain relative calls, do some deep breathing exercises before you talk to them. These small shifts end up leading to big changes over time.

Chapter 2: Your Purpose and Positivity

Most people have no idea what they would like to do with their life. Some assume that it will eventually become clear to them as they get older, once they complete school, or once they're married. But the truth is that you may still have no clue, even after going through these big changes. Part of the difficulty with this question is the idea of "purpose" in life.

Many of us have a ton of baggage attached to this idea. We may believe that it's such a huge deal, or that without it, we're doomed to live a life of misery. Needless to say, this puts a bit too much pressure on the quest to find our life purpose. Try to approach the situation with a fresh perspective and an attitude of curiosity.

Questions for Finding Your Purpose

Finding your purpose should be an interesting, fun process and not something you dread or feel is an obligation. Feel free to mix and match these questions, or even add some of your own.

1. What Would You Do if Money Were No Object?

How would you spend your life if you already had all of your financial concerns covered? Perhaps you'd spend your days painting, helping other people through volunteer work, or golfing with your friends. Whatever this passion is, it's time to dedicate more of your life to it. It may become your life purpose, or it may just give you an outlet for relaxation and happiness. Either way is conducive to finding out what your purpose in life is.

2. Can You Handle Sacrifice for Your Dream?

The fact is that everything worthwhile in life involves sacrifice and comes at a cost. How much sacrifice can you deal with to reach your goal? Knowing the answer to this question will allow you to figure out how realistic one pursuit is in comparison with another. Here are some examples of sacrifices you may have to deal with if you pursue a specific path:

- If you want to be an entrepreneur, are you ready to face rejection time and time again?

- Do you want to be a writer without ever facing critique?

- Are you ready to give hours and hours of your day to your interest?

If these negative potential outcomes are enough to turn you away from something, then the goal is not your true path.

3. What Did You Love as a Child?

Certain things never change in a person. Oftentimes, what your favorite pastime was as a child can tell you a lot about what your life purpose could be now. For instance, maybe you loved to write stories as a kid and spent days doing it for the sheer joy and immersion it brought you. Odds are, whatever this interest was for you as a kid, you don't do nearly as much anymore. This could be because we've become self-conscious about our interest or that we only think things are worthwhile if they bring financial gain.

One of your first steps for reconnecting with your life purpose should be revisiting whatever it was your childhood self loved to spend hours doing. As a kid, do you think you would have stopped doing something just because you didn't think it was profitable or good enough? No, you would have done what you loved just because you loved it. Reconnect with that part of you.

4. When Do You Forget Time Exists?

Everyone has had an experience of the flow state, that state of mind that is so immersive that you forget to eat dinner. Maybe you get so immersed in coding that you don't leave your apartment for an entire day, which could be a big clue as to what your life purpose could be. Even an activity that is not typically thought of as "productive" such as gaming, could give you a hint as to what's important to you.

- **The Qualities Behind the Activity:** Taking the example of gaming, if you spend all day immersed in this activity, it could point to several traits or interests in you. You could thrive on a competitive atmosphere, for goal-setting, or general improvement in life conditions.

- **Applying those Qualities:** When you can apply the obsession you feel for self-competition and improvement to your passion or business, this will take you very far. For you, this could mean efficient organization, teaching, fixing problems, or something related to your social life. Whatever the case, make sure you are looking at the principles behind the activities to find what it is that makes it so addictive and compelling to you. These principles can be applied in other areas, too.

5. Being Okay with Vulnerability

When you're new to something, or rather inexperienced, you are probably going to be clueless at first. That's just the way it goes. And to be bad at something means you might end up embarrassing yourself and feeling vulnerable, probably over and over again. It's completely normal for people to try to avoid embarrassment, because it doesn't feel very good. But if everyone were to avoid the potential of doing something embarrassing, they would never reach new heights!

- **Acceptance:** You have to teach yourself to be okay with being vulnerable. At this moment, there's probably something you'd love to be learning about or pursuing, but reasons behind why you don't. These reasons are likely something you repeat to yourself on a regular basis. Often, these reasons have to do with potential reactions of other people to what you might do. Do you worry about being judged by your peers if you fail? Do you worry about your parents not accepting your new path? Then you're focusing on the wrong factors.

Accepting the possibility that others may not agree with your path and that it matters enough to you to stick with is the key here. Everything great on this planet is unconventional, unique, and to some people, shocking. So, you have to go against what others think to do anything amazing. This can be very frightening due to the fear of looking foolish or getting embarrassed. But what is the price to pay for ignoring your inner calling? Is it worth it to suppress yourself just to avoid a bit of embarrassment or scorn?

- **Seeing Your Newbie Status as a Strength:** A lot of times, experts or people who are very experienced in a certain field get stuck in concepts and don't know where to go. They find it hard to think creatively. For this reason, being new to something can actually be an advantage. You're seeing everything in the field with new eyes. This can apply to anything from business, to playing an instrument, to general self-improvement tasks. Someone who has a fresh, blank perspective can often see connections where others struggle.

6. Find Out How You Can Help

As I mentioned before, we are social beings and
helping each other is important. Unless you live under
a rock, you already know that the world has no
shortage of current problems to focus on. What
speaks most to you in this sea of issues? In order to be
happy and satisfied in life, it's important to be a part
of something bigger that benefits others. Here are
some ideas for getting involved:

- **Helping the Homeless:** Do you feel a tug on
  your heartstrings any time you see a homeless
  person on the street? Don't ignore this! That
  could mean that you would get a lot out of
  volunteering your time at a shelter or finding

other ways to help your fellow humans in need.

- **Writing about Issues:** Our education system isn't very great, domestic violence is a problem, and mental healthcare could use some improvement. All of these are issues you could be helping to spread the word about. Do you have a blog or a writing talent? Start using it to get information about something you care about.

Find something to care about and put your energies into helping. This won't mean you'll fix the issue on your own, but you will feel that you've made a difference, however small. And feeling connected to something and knowing you're making small, positive changes can do wonders for your self-esteem and will likely get you a little closer to finding your true purpose in life.

7. What Do You Want to be Remembered For?

Imagine that you just got a cancer diagnosis and know that you'll die within half a year. Yes, I know, it's not fun to think about dying and can be a scary thought. But this can give you many practical benefits. One of them is that it helps you discern what matters most to you in your life from what is pure, useless distraction. A lot of people wouldn't know how to answer this question, so if you have a little difficulty thinking of something on the spot, don't worry. Give it some thought before you find the answer. Here are other related questions to ponder:

- **What Will You Leave Behind?** How will others remember you once you leave this earth? Will it be mostly positive things or negative things? What can you do to make sure that you're remembered in a positive light when you leave this earth? If you can't think of anything but people saying impressive stuff about what you owned when you were alive, you probably aren't digging deep enough.

- **What are Your Values?** If you're having trouble deciding how you want people to remember you, it could be that you aren't sure what your values are or what matters most to you in life. This leaves you open to the danger of taking on the priorities of other people and allowing them to direct your life instead of you. This path can never lead to true happiness or fulfilling relationships.

- **The Writing Test:** If you *still* don't know what your values or purpose are, it's time to do the writing test to get a little deeper. Get a piece of paper (or an empty text document on your computer, though actually writing with a pen feels more personal) and write at the top "What am I on this earth for?" Does this sound dramatic? Good! Now just start writing. At first, you may find that it's hard to know what to say but keep going. Keep digging and questioning until the words start flowing naturally. This should give you some clarity.

Figuring out what your purpose is means finding out what cause or goal you can be a part of that is larger than you or the people around you. It's not about earning \$50,000 more per year or finally dating that specific person; it's bigger than that. How would your time be best spent? How can you make it more meaningful? If nothing comes to mind, you need to get out there and experiment more to find it. And that brings me to something else that will help you immensely along the way...

The Power of Positivity

Positive thinking is a bit of a buzzword these days, but what does it really mean? Although it's a no-brainer that most of us want to be more positive than negative, it's also a term that is so widely used it's lost a bit of its original meaning. But research is starting to reveal that it's about more than being upbeat and in a good, happy mood. Positive thinking can bring true value to your life, strengthen your self-discipline, and lead to all sorts of other useful skills in work and your personal life.

The results that positive thinking can have on your professional life, relationships, and even health is currently being observed by experts in psychology. Frederickson, a researcher of positive psychology at North Carolina university has found a few surprising new facts about how positive thinking can impact your skills in life. These useful bits of information can be applied practically to your life and self-discipline goals, no matter what they are specifically focused on. Here are some ideas from her research.

The Impact of Negativity

Science has known for a while that negative feelings prompt the brain to perform something specific.

When you encounter a potentially life-threatening situation, you get out of there as fast as you can. Suddenly, nothing else in your surroundings matters whatsoever in comparison. You will be focused completely on the threat, the state of mind created by the threat, and how to save yourself. Even if you do have a wide variety of choices available to you in the moment, your mind will narrow its focus and hone in on only one.

- **How This Developed:** In the early days of human development, this is a trait that saved our skins countless times, no doubt. Encountering a wild predator is one example of a scenario where that particular brain function would have come in handy. However, this is the modern world and that tendency can get in the way a lot of the time, rather than help us. Our brains are programmed to feel a threat (however insignificant in actuality) and turn the world off, limiting options and creating tunnel vision.

- **Examples of Negativity Tunnel Vision:** Imagine that you just got into an argument with your best friend and had to go to work immediately after. Odds are, in this situation, you would have a very hard time focusing on work and instead would be replaying the scenario over and over in your mind. Or what about those days where you know you have a task list a foot long and can't seem to prompt yourself to get started on any of the items on the list? In each scenario, your negative thoughts are closing you off to thinking creatively or seeing other choices.

The Impacts of Positivity

Now it's time to compare this with what happens in your brain when you are having positive thoughts.

- **The Experiment:** Fredrickson looked at the way positive emotions impacted the brain in an experiment where subjects were divided into groups and shown various video clips. The first group was shown images that prompted joyful feelings, while the second group looked at clips that made them feel content. A third group was the "neutral" group that was shown clips that had no emotion attached to them. Finally, there were two more groups shown feelings of fear and anger, respectively.

- **The Results:** After the groups were shown these clips, all of the participants were asked to envision a scenario that would prompt similar feelings and to record on a piece of paper how they would react. Each of them were given a sheet of paper with 20 sentences that began with "I would like to…" The group members that viewed images related to anger and fear recorded fewer responses. The group members who viewed content and joyful images listed many more actions they wanted to take compared to both the negative groups and the neutral group.

- **What Does This Show?** This experiment showed that when someone is feeling love, contentment, and joyful feelings, they will have more ideas and see more options. These were some of the first scientific findings that showed that positive thinking can broaden possibilities and have a mind-opening impact. But that's not all...

Positive Thinking and Other Skills

Positive thinking leads to even more advantages than great feelings and more possibilities. Actually, the greatest advantage that positive thinking brings is a stronger ability to develop resources and build skills that will help you later on in your life.

- **Unexpected Advantages:** Enjoyable habits can bring unexpected benefits. For instance, a kid who spends a lot of time outside with his friends, climbing trees, builds up the skills of athletic movement, social communication, and creative reasoning. In this example, the positive feelings of joy and play help the child to develop skills that will help them in other areas of life later on. And these traits end up lasting a lot longer than the positive feelings that prompted them in the first place.

- **A Solid Foundation:** Later in the future, the positive foundation of social skills could lead to a prosperous career in team management. The joy that brought about the creation and exploration of new traits isn't there anymore, while the lasting impacts are. Positive feelings open you up to new possibilities, bringing you brand new resources and skills and giving more value to unrelated and often unexpected areas in life. This is the opposite of what negative feelings do. So, the next question is, how can you be more positive in life to get these great benefits?

How to Think More Positively

What actionable steps can you take to improve your skill of positive thinking? To start with, any action or activity that brings you feelings of love, contentment, or joy can help with this. You likely already have a few ideas in mind for that. It could be playing piano, hanging out with your spouse, or cooking. Here are some other general tasks to focus on that will bring you more positive emotions and benefits:

- **Positive Journaling:** Do you keep a journal? If not, it's time to start. Not only will this help you develop self-discipline by ensuring you stick with your goal of writing each day, but it can help you become more positive. In one study, a group of 90 participants were split into two different groups. One group was asked to write each day, for three days, on something intensely positive. The other group wrote on a neutral topic. A few months later, the participants who did positive journaling for three days had to visit the doctor less frequently and reported better moods and fewer sicknesses.

- **Make Time for Play:** Make some time in your life for playing. The average person schedules appointments, events, and meetings, so why not pencil in some playtime for yourself? Have you ever set aside an hour just for experimentation and exploration? Do you ever carve out some time specifically for fun and enjoyment? Happiness is at least as important as that work conference you have on your calendar, yet a lot of people don't act like this is true. Make time for this in your life and you will reap the wonderful benefits of positivity.

- **Gratitude Lists:** Looking for things to be grateful for is another great way to increase the amount of positivity present in your life. This can be done first thing in the morning or right before going to sleep (or if you really want to go above and beyond, both!) and can be done mentally or on paper. Make a list of what you are grateful for in that moment, no matter how seemingly small or big. Even if it's something like "The sun is shining today," that's a good start.

The Illusion of Putting Off Happiness

Most of us believe that success is what leads to happiness. And it's true that certain situations can bring you more joy. But having this perspective as a default might be preventing you from experiencing more happiness in your life. Do you often think that as soon as you make a specific change in your life you will finally be happy? Or maybe you think that once you buy a certain item, you'll feel joy again. How often does it actually happen? Chances are, you feel great for a short while and then it fades.

All of us are guilty of doing this to some degree. But the research on positivity we just covered should be enough to show you that happiness can be a great precursor for building the habits that will lead to success. So, happiness is not always the result of what you achieve but can also be the reason for your success. Happy people build new skills, gain new successes because of them, then feel even more joy, repeating this upward spiral ad infinitum.

Start making time to feel more positive emotions in life, by playing a sport, doing something creative, or just spending more time with your loved ones. This will lower your stress levels, make you smile, and even improve your self-discipline. Positive emotions and creative exploration open the door for reflection and growth in your life. The key to sticking with your chosen path is self-discipline, and the burden will feel much lighter with a positive approach.

Chapter 3: Dealing with Failure and Increasing Productivity

When it comes to the subject of failure, our own pride can be our worst enemy. Once events in life begin going the wrong way, we might go into survival mode, trying to maintain composure and possibly even lying to ourselves. But these common reactions, like clinging to what's changing, or denial, can ruin our ability to grow and adapt to changes in our lives. It can be extremely difficult to admit it to ourselves when we've messed up and try to fix it. Or we might hastily scramble to fix things, only to make them worse through a lack of forethought or careful planning.

Another common reaction to personal failure or mistakes is to lie to ourselves, pretend they didn't happen, or act like the mistake was a far lesser deal than it really was. We might be so nervous about what happened that we miss out on a real opportunity to fix it. So, all of this begs the question, how can we successfully adapt to change and deal with failure with grace?

How to Adapt Successfully

In our complicated world, it's necessary to keep an experimental, adaptive mentality and approach in order to reach success. We also need this attitude to develop a strong sense of self-discipline and excel at our goals. It's impossible to predict ahead of time whether the ideas we have or the risks we take will pay off once we launch them. Oftentimes, failure is inevitable, but there's good news! There is a way to fail in a productive manner. Here are the guidelines for failing productively:

1. Mix It Up

When you put all your eggs in one basket, a single failure can be very devastating. For this reason, among others, it's good to mix it up. Just as you should diversify your investments to avoid big losses, you should also have a wide variety of interests and plans in terms of business or your personal life. Even when it comes to hobbies, constantly looking for fresh ideas will help you see that a failure in one area isn't the end of the world, and you'll always have something else to fall back on.

2. Be Honest with Yourself

The next step for dealing with failure with poise is being completely honest with yourself about it when it does occur. Mistakes become much worse when you dwell on them or constantly beat yourself up over what happened. In order to rise above this common reaction, it's crucial to learn to recognize when you have failed. One way to recognize failure is to constantly ask for feedback from your peers. Asking someone you trust how you're doing and for honest critique can help you see a bit more clearly.

3. Get Rid of Attachments

This is hard when you're dealing with matters that are important to you, but handling failure in the right way calls for maintaining a healthy sense of non-attachment to outcomes. This doesn't mean you won't care; it just means that a single loss won't completely devastate you and throw your life off track. Stay adaptable, look for ways to grow, and always have a plan B.

4. Ask What You Can Learn

The best way to handle failure with ease and get more out of it is to ask yourself what you can learn from what happened. You may consider a low sales month at your job a failure, but dwelling on that and telling yourself you're no good isn't going to help. Instead, ask yourself what you did differently that may have contributed to the streak of low sales. Then ask yourself what you can do to make it better. Construct an action plan and you're already on your way to being productive with your failures!

Mastering the Art of Self-Discipline

Any master gets amazing at their art or trade by consistent practice, an attitude of devotion, and an openness to learning more. This is the approach required to become a master of self-discipline. Here are some practices that will help you gain an unshakeable and reliable sense of discipline that you can always fall back on no matter what happens.

Do It, Even When You Don't Feel Like It

Procrastination is an issue that most of us are familiar with. We usually procrastinate by telling ourselves that we simply don't feel like doing the task right now. It could be that the task is intimidating, confusing, or difficult in some way and makes us feel uncomfortable. This could lead you to seek a distracting or pleasant activity to occupy yourself with instead. The amazing thing is, in this mentality, we can find endless ways to occupy ourselves that help us avoid the task we know we should be doing.

Before you can start trimming your nails, checking Facebook, or watering your plants to avoid the task, begin the task immediately. Right when your mind starts to chime in and try to convince you to do something else, just do it anyway. Oftentimes, the fear of the task itself is far worse than the action itself.

Start Exercising Every Day

This is one of the greatest ways to build self-discipline because it's something that nearly every one of us has put off in one way or another. Exercise can feel hard when you aren't used to it, so we distract ourselves with something else, putting it off until "tomorrow" every day. But this can be seen as an ordinary part of maintaining your health, like brushing your teeth and eating. Show up to your exercise even when you're tired or don't feel like it. Odds are, you won't ever feel perfectly ready to do it, but you'll never regret a completed workout.

Learn to Recognize Real Hunger

Most people get anxious when they're hungry and reach for the closest thing to eat, even if it's junk, but the truth is that a little hunger isn't bad for you. In fact, many times, we use our hunger as a distraction tactic to avoid doing what we should be doing. So next time you feel the urge to reach for a bag of potato chips, analyze your hunger and see if it's real or an excuse to distract yourself. This is just an exercise that will show you that it's possible to be more conscious about your automatic decisions. This could also help you lose weight if that's a goal you have.

Face the Issue

Most of us avoid thinking about problems in our lives. Perhaps this is avoiding a financial problem, putting off a big project, or ignoring the fact that you need to get healthier. These realities can be hard to face because again, they make us uncomfortable and we'd rather ignore them. But try developing a new attitude towards problems in your life. Next time you notice an obstacle, see it as a different path. Acknowledge the path, find out as much as you can about it, and learn how to navigate. This will make you much stronger and more disciplined as a person.

Be Direct in Conversation

Make it a goal to have uncomfortable conversations. Most people avoid them because they can feel a little awkward or scary. But doing this just leads to problems including avoidance, resentment, and fights.

Instead of succumbing to the temptation of avoiding an awkward conversation at work or with your loved one, try to raise the issue in a compassionate, gentle and empathetic way. Ask them if you can talk, and then share your feelings. As long as you make sure you don't sound defensive and you do plenty of listening, it should go smoothly. Avoiding problems doesn't make them disappear, so get in the habit of facing your problems head on.

Look for the Good

Discipline is all about realizing that you don't need a huge, fancy award for everything you do. Getting things done is rewarding enough in itself. For example, you can learn how to relish going on a walk every morning instead of telling yourself that you can eat cake later if you do it. Or you can learn how to enjoy healthier foods instead of obsessively counting calories or dieting. Oftentimes, when you know how to look, the reward is in the new activity itself.

Remind Yourself of Intentions

One common challenge people undergo is staying true to their habit once the initial motivation wears off, as it inevitably does. It's not that hard to stick with something for a week, but it can get a little more challenging during the second or third week. Most people don't become masters of self-discipline because they quit before they get over the initial hump and don't give themselves enough time to establish momentum. Try committing to just one tiny habit for 60 days, even if it's only 5 to 10 minutes per day.

No matter what comes up, do this new activity each and every day at the same time and give yourself reminders on your phone or post-it notes around the house so you remember. Keep track of your progress on your calendar so you can see and celebrate your success. You can gradually add more and more positive, small habits. Before you know it, you will do these new habits without even giving them a second thought.

Using Self-Discipline to Become More Productive

There is no shortage of hacks, systems, articles, and tips on the internet that are designed to help with productivity and efficiency. But a lot of people who read blogs and books about productivity still find that they struggle to use the tools effectively. No matter how great the system is, an email organization tool won't do the work for you. No tricks or tips for becoming better at budgeting will think for you. The main issue for people who have a hard time with productivity is not an inability to learn new systems, but a lack of discipline.

The New Muscle

You can think of self-discipline as a new muscle that you haven't worked out before. At first, it's going to be a little tough, but it will get stronger the more you use it. Building your self-discipline from the point of view of productivity is being able to just do what you need to do. Depending on the field it pertains to, self-discipline can mean a variety of different things. If you're a musician, it can mean picking up your guitar every afternoon, even when you'd rather watch TV. If you're dedicated to learning a language, it means dedicating time each day to practicing.

Creating Results

But the most very helpful definition you can use for self-discipline is a tool to create results in your life. Everyone has ideas, but it's only the people who can get themselves to act that get any good results from them. Coming up with a system for organizing or processing email won't matter if you don't actually implement the new system when you have a chance.

Tips for Disciplined Productivity

But this knowledge is only the first step. Knowing something does not mean you will be productive. Only implementation can guarantee results. As stated, anyone can have a concept in their head, but it's only the people who know how to make themselves act on their ideas that will enjoy the success we all look up to and crave. Here are some tips for getting there.

1. Start Out Small

If you've never been able to bring about small ideas in your life, then it's going to be hard to make something huge happen immediately. Sure, it may work for someone every once in a while to attack a momentous goal and succeed at it right away, but for the rest of us, starting out small is going to be the best course of action. Let's return to the comparison of being disciplined to using a new muscle.

If you've never worked out your arms before, do you think you'd be able to lift an extremely heavy item?

No. And you won't be able to build a successful business or valuable, worthwhile habit overnight either. Here are some ideas for small changes you can begin implanting today:

- **Drinking More Water:** If you have a goal of losing weight, for example, it won't happen overnight. You are going to have junk food cravings for a while. But you can start with a small change like replacing your soda with lemon water or drinking your coffee without sugar. This can make a bigger difference in your weight than you realize.

- **Making Small Agreements:** If you're struggling with productivity or self-discipline, another good place to start is by making small appointments that you must stick to no matter what happens. This can be calling your mom every week, or something related to your business.

- **Unplug and Recharge:** More and more, people are starting to realize the benefit of turning off their computers and phones to allow their minds to rest. This small change can pave the way for a lot more productivity because you'll get the break you need. Try starting with just an hour of being phone-free per day, then work your way up.

Now, these changes may seem small or insignificant on their own, but they will add up to huge changes over time. And more importantly, you will learn that you have it in you to change any time you want to. With these small changes, your sense of self-discipline will slowly rise. Before you know it, you'll be tackling far bigger changes and feeling like a brand-new person!

2. Check Your Expectations

It would be a mistake to expect a weak muscle to be as strong as a muscle you're accustomed to using on a regular basis, and this also applies to your self-discipline muscle. Make sure that you aren't giving yourself unrealistic expectations or this will be much harder than it has to be.

3. Stay Accountable

When an individual has atrophied muscles and can no longer use them, they have to take intense therapy to rebuild strength. They must start out small and gradually increase the load until their muscles work again. This can also happen to your self-discipline, so you have to find a way to stay accountable. Whether this means signing up for a group or finding a partner who you can check in with, accountability is going to keep you on the right track towards your goals and keep you disciplined.

Try finding a person who is encouraging and helpful, who will be present in your daily life and wants to aid you in your goals. If you're trying to form a specific habit for professional reasons, then it can be a work colleague. But habits that have to do with your home life might be a little more complicated. If your goal is to quit smoking, for example, you may need a friend or relative to help you stay accountable. It's even better if this individual has the same goal as you, so you can lean on each other. If you don't know anyone in your life, check out groups online for support.

4. Give Yourself Challenges

For most people, routine can be the biggest enemy of success. This leads to sitting on the couch night after night or spending way too much time scrolling Facebook instead of pursuing worthwhile activities. But getting stuck in a rut like this will ensure that nothing new or exciting ever happens to us. And that's a serious issue. Contrary to popular belief, passion and enthusiasm are the byproducts of taking action, not the reasons for it.

- **Try New Things:** Figuring out what you care most about in life is going to take some time. And until you know, you'll probably be a pro at finding countless excuses for not pursuing more worthwhile activities. The fact is that no one knows how they will feel about something unless they try.

- **If TV Disappeared:** Ask yourself what you would spend your days doing if the television and Facebook suddenly disappeared and you had to leave your house each day to do something. Would you go back to school? Learn how to salsa dance? Take up snowboarding? It's time to stop putting off these activities and take action now.

Chapter 4: Meditation and Focus in Self-Discipline

The average person thinks that meditation is a mystical or difficult activity, but the truth is that it's very simple. Meditation can improve your self-discipline and focus in amazing ways. There are countless techniques for meditation, but it's best to start out with something simple at first. No one is good at meditation when they start out, but that's the point of practicing. You will soon learn as you continue practicing that you can stay with an activity, even if it seems hard.

Simple Beginner Meditation

You don't have to be a Buddhist to meditate. You can even start getting into the swing of it now. Throughout the day, start reminding yourself to focus on your breath and clear your mind. You can even set reminders on your phone. Go as long as you can focus on your breath and noticing every thought that comes up. Once you've done this for a few days, it's time to move onto sitting meditation:

1. **Sit Down:** The first step is to simply sit down. Some are flexible enough to sit cross-legged on the floor on a cushion comfortably, but most people will need to use a chair. If sitting in a chair with a straight back is uncomfortable for you, you can lie down, but try not to fall asleep.

2. **Keep Your Eyes Closed:** Now, gently close your eyes and keep them shut for the duration of this practice. Start breathing normally, but maybe a little deeper than you usually would. Try to breathe through the belly, allowing your abdomen to rise and fall, instead of through the

chest.

3. **Start with 2 Minutes:** When you first begin
   this practice, start with setting your alarm for
   only 2 minutes. This may sound like a pointless
   amount of time, but it's important to slowly
   ease into this. As you get comfortable with
   these 2-minute intervals, you can begin
   working your way up to longer periods.

Most people will get frustrated when they learn to
meditate because they will find that their mind is
extremely loud and active, trying to pull them away
from sitting calmly. This is something you should
expect and plan for, because it happens to everyone.
This is normal and don't let it upset you. Just stay
with it and be patient and it will get easier and easier.
Soon, you may even find yourself looking forward to

your meditation sessions when you notice how much calmer and more focused they make you.

There's No Such Thing as "Trying"

When we are "trying" to get something done, we may use limited time as an excuse not to complete anything. Perhaps it's a work project that you're trying to do, but you keep telling yourself that you only have a half hour of free time and that's not enough to get anything substantial done. Under this logic, watching TV or doing chores sounds like the more sensible thing to do. You tell yourself that you are "trying" to do something, when a lot of the time, that's simply not the case. You are either doing something or you aren't.

- **Avoidance:** Many times, trying is our way of choosing avoidance because we're afraid of something. Maybe we're afraid to change, afraid to disappoint our parents, or afraid of judgment from our peers for doing something different. Claiming to ourselves that we are trying is a convenient method for avoiding a commitment while pretending that you have committed. It's an avoidance tactic.

- **Change Your Language:** You must realize that the language of "trying" will make you fall short, because trying is not action. It's procrastination. Pay attention to the words you choose to use and keep in mind that you can either choose to do something or choose not to. Own your decisions. Be honest with yourself about why you choose or don't choose to do something.

- **Admit when You Don't Want to:** Instead of telling yourself that you're trying when you aren't, instead admit that you don't want to do something. This will either help you realize that you can still choose to get the task done, or help you come up with a plan for a better time to do it. Be real with yourself so you can perfect your sense of self-discipline.

Chapter 5: Avoiding Burnout and Overcoming Resistance

The Pareto principle, also known as the 80/20 rule is very effective for better time management. This principle states that 80 percent of your results in life are going to come from 20 percent of the actions you take. This realization will help you change your process of setting and achieving goals. This principle was named after Vilfredo Pareto in the year 1895 when he noticed there were about 20 percent of people who succeeded, while the rest fell into the bottom 80 percent.

He soon realized that almost all activity in economics also adhered to this pattern. 20 percent of people controlled 80 percent of wealth in Italy then. And this principle can be applied to many different situations for us today. You can use this to prioritize your days and tasks and become more productive and disciplined with your goals. So how exactly does the principle work? If you make a list of 10 items you need to get done, two items on the list are more important than the remaining 8 items. But the sad truth is that many people put off the top 20 percent of task items that matter the most, focusing instead on the other 8 items that don't matter much and won't bring them real success.

Using the Pareto Principle for Goals

You can use this principle for more effective goal-setting and to enhance your discipline. Follow these simple rules and you will be successfully applying the 80/20 principle and thriving as a result.

- **Make a List:** Begin by writing your 10 most important goals of the moment. Then figure out which one of them you would choose if you had to select the goal that will have the biggest payoff in your current situation. Place a number 1 next to that task. Next, choose the follow-up goal in terms of importance. You will soon realize that once you've completed this exercise that you've identified the 20 percent that will be most worthwhile. Focus on those before the others. Here are some more steps to help you along the way.

- **Tackle the Hardest Goal First:** The world is full of people who look like they're always busy but who hardly get anything done. That's because they are usually busying themselves with tasks that aren't very important, putting off the harder and more important goals. The valuable activities are usually the harder ones, but they will lead to a greater payoff. Just tackle the bigger goals first and the rest of your day will be a breeze. Resist the urge to do the easier tasks first.

- **Keep Your Eyes Ahead:** Although it's good to break your goals into smaller and more manageable tasks, you should have one major goal that keeps you motivated and disciplined to continue. This will be your fuel for the days that you'd rather lie around and be lazy. If your goal is to become the top CEO of your company, print out a photo of a successful businessman that you will look at every day. This can represent your vision of success. If you want to move into your dream home within five years, set your phone background as a picture of a similar house. These tricks will help you keep your major goal in mind at all times, even when the going gets tough.

Tips for Preventing Burnout

Although self-discipline sounds like being tough on yourself, it also involves knowing when to take a break. Without them, you will eventually burn out. Burnout gets in the way of your ability to think clearly and creatively, making you think in more rigid ways. This is what happens when you work overtime every single week and don't make time for relaxation or de-stressing. Here are some tips you can follow to prevent burnout, so you can stay on task with your goals.

Make Time for Creativity

What is your favorite creative activity? It could be singing, painting, or dancing. Whatever it is, make some time for it and don't neglect the enjoyment of the activity because you believe it isn't productive. Even when you can't apply that creative skill to your professional life, this outlet will help you de-stress and recover from your workload, keeping you motivated and engaged.

Get Up Often

If you, like so many other modern-day people, sit at a desk all day, you need to make sure you're standing up and moving around often. Most people stay sitting at their desks even when they're on break, operating under the illusion that the more immersed in their work they are, the better off they'll be. But the truth is that you aren't a machine and you need a break. Our bodies are built to move around, not sit sedentary all day. Try to stand up and stretch or take a quick walk around the office at least once an hour, but even more than that is better if you can.

Don't Avoid Others

Support is important for human beings, and more and more of them have no one to confide in about their personal issues, according to research. It's true that the more stressed out or exhausted we fell, the more we want to be alone, oftentimes. But the fact is that that is the last thing you should do in that situation. Make time for social interaction, even when you don't feel like it. You will be surprised at how big of a difference it makes in how you feel.

Kill the People-Pleaser

But just as important as it is to make time for social interaction with other people, it's equally crucial to make sure we're listening to our own inner guidance instead of others when it matters the most. Many of us say "yes" to people at work or in our personal lives just because it's easier to avoid confrontation, even when we're exhausted and need some time to unwind alone. Notice when you do this and try to get rid of the habit of being a people-pleaser.

Be Solution-Oriented

We already dedicated a section in the book to the importance of positivity, and this is a somewhat related point. Positivity makes you more creative and resilient, enabling you to think in terms of solutions instead of avoidance. The more you tune into positivity when you're on the brink of burning out, the more you will learn how to relax and recognize when you need a break. If your main goal is being productive at work, it pays to remind yourself that you won't be very successful if you keep going until your positivity (and as a result, your creativity and innovative thinking) has completely run out. Take the time to rest and recharge your batteries.

Overcoming Resistance

People are afraid of change. We are creatures of habit and like to stay in our familiar routines and bubbles without being disturbed. In fact, this is so true that people often dislike when *others* change too, even if it has nothing to do with them. Do you struggle with sticking by your heart's desires because you're afraid of what others will say? The truth is that people like stability and homeostasis, and they want you to remain predictable. But is that a reason to throw away your values and settle for a life you don't really want?

When you change in real ways, it will force the people around you to change too because they'll have to find new ways to respond to your shifts. A lot of people don't like this and will resist it. They might try to talk you out of a new job or a new look and won't be interested in hearing your logical reasoning behind your choice. How can you handle these reactions, both from other people and yourself? Should you give up on changing and stay the same old predictable you? Absolutely not! Here are some preparations you can make to handle resistance better.

1. Know Your Reasons

When your mind (or mother) begins to give you reasons why you shouldn't try something new, have your main motivation in mind. Don't allow this truth to waver at all and keep your mind on it no matter what happens. Be ready to defend yourself, if necessary, but don't go picking a fight. When you know exactly why you're doing something, words to the contrary have no bearing on you. If you are confident in your choices, the opinions of others (or of your own insecure side) won't be able to change your mind.

2. Have a Comeback Ready

Plan out what you will say if someone tries to talk you out of something you've already decided on. This comeback could be funny, logical, or whatever feels right to you. Imagine that you're about to make a career change and pursue the job you really want, but that you're leaving your old career behind and want to tell your parents about it. Think of what the likeliest response will be to your news, ("But you've had that job for 10 years, it would be foolish to quit now!") and prepare what you will say ahead of time. Make it clear that you aren't looking to be talked out of your choice.

3. Make New Friends Who Get it

It can be hard to follow a specific path if you aren't surrounded by people who understand it. If you don't have any friends who can support your new goal, it may be time to seek out some new ones. Join a club that revolves around your interest, or even an internet forum where you can discuss it. Support is crucial. Instead of seeking out encouraging words from the

people who don't approve of your new way of acting,
save your updates for people who do.

4. Share Your Progress (When Asked)

Odds are, when you begin to show that sense of satisfaction and happiness from your new changes, the people in your life will want some of what you're having. If you can tell that someone wants more information on how you made your change, be there to offer insight and tips. Don't preach to them about it, but answer questions if they ask. Change doesn't happen overnight, but you can be a good resource for someone if they are interested in taking a similar path or pursuing their own goal.

5. Be Tough

There are going to be instances where this new path you've chosen feels lonely and difficult. But this has to be your motivation to continue. When you push through these hard times, you have a chance to make real, lasting changes. This is what real self-discipline is all about; staying on your path even when it isn't easy. It's what separates the amazing achievers from the average Joes. Make a list of all the reasons why you are going after whatever your specific goal is. Any time you're struggling, review the list so you can remind yourself why you're doing what you're doing.

6. Remember That It's a Process

Don't ever forget that success is not just a single step, but an ongoing process. As soon as you achieve what you wanted more than anything in one area, there will be something else worth going after before you know it. Success is a long, varied path that you must be truly

dedicated to in order to succeed.

Now you have all the tools you need to succeed in life.

If you stick to the steps in this book, you will

experience a total, radical shift in your self-discipline.

With this information, you can become as fit as you

want, find a new career, or build a beautiful

relationship with your partner. You can apply these

basic principles to your life no matter what your goal

is.

Chapter 6 Final Thoughts

Thanks for picking up *Self-Discipline and Mental Toughness: A Guide to Developing Your Grit and Increasing Your Productivity*. I hope that this book gave you the inspiration you need to become a more self-disciplined individual and as a result, achieve your deepest dreams in life.

Life is full of problems and challenges along the path to achievement and success. But to get past these, you must be persistent, persevere, and develop a strong identity of self-discipline. This skill will give you healthy self-esteem, confidence in all you do, and satisfaction and general life happiness, as well. If you ignore or neglect to develop self-discipline, on the other hand, you could be looking at loss, failures, bad relationships, and low self-worth.

Whether your goal is to overcome a negative habit, improve your study habits, exercise more often, or rise to the top in your professional field, you need this skill. There are plenty of books out there on the market about self-discipline, so thank you for choosing this one. If you found it helpful, please take the time to leave it a review on Amazon! Thanks again and good luck out there.

Furthermore, the transmission, duplication or reproduction of any of the following work, including precise information, will be considered an illegal act, irrespective whether it is done electronically or in print. The legality extends to creating a secondary or tertiary copy of the work or a recorded copy and is only allowed with express written consent of the Publisher. All additional rights are reserved.

The information in the following pages is broadly considered to be a truthful and accurate account of facts, and as such any inattention, use or misuse of the information in question by the reader will render any resulting actions solely under their purview. There are no scenarios in which the publisher or the original author of this work can be in any fashion deemed liable for any hardship or damages that may befall them after undertaking information described herein.

Additionally, the information found on the following pages is intended for informational purposes only and should thus be considered, universal. As befitting its nature, the information presented is without assurance regarding its continued validity or interim quality. Trademarks that mentioned are done without written consent and can in no way be considered an endorsement from the trademark holder.

Description

In *Self-Discipline and Mental Toughness: A Guide to Developing Your Grit and Increasing Your Productivity,* you will learn:

- **Motivation vs. Discipline:** Most of us seek motivation, but what exactly is this quality? Although it can be a useful tool or mindset for achieving greatness, it's not always as reliable as you might think. Chapter one will tell you what type of motivation is most reliable and also how self-discipline can, in many cases, be superior to simple motivation.

- **Finding Your Purpose:** What do you want to be remembered for when you die? What is your deepest purpose in life? These are tough questions for most of us. Chapter two will walk you through these questions, and more, so you can get to the root of your values and goals and live a more meaningful life.

- **How to Handle Failure:** Did you know that failure can be a great advantage on the path to success? It's all in how you approach it mentally. In chapter three, and throughout the rest of the book, we will illustrate how and why this is the case, so you can reframe your perspective on failure and mistakes.

- **Meditation and Focus:** If you spend a fair amount of time online, you may already know about all of the great health benefits of meditation. In chapter four, we will cover how meditation can improve your focus and self-discipline, as well as give you specific instructions for how to start meditating today.

- **Avoiding Burnout:** Burnout is what happens when you don't give yourself a break and you work too hard. There are tips and techniques for avoiding this unfortunate state, which we will cover in chapter five. In this chapter, we will also go over how to overcome resistance to change, both in others and yourself.

As you can see, this book is full of valuable tips that can bring serious changes to your life. If you're ready to stop making excuses and procrastinating, it's about time you learned how to develop self-discipline. This guide will help you do that.

Meditation for Beginners

A Beginners Guide to Finding Tranquility & Relieving Stress, Anxiety, and Depression

By Martin Brandt

Contents

Introduction: What is Meditation?

Congratulations on downloading your personal copy of *Meditation for Beginners: How to Meditate and Find Tranquility, Relieve Stress and Anxiety, and Depression.* Thank you for doing so.

Meditation has been used loosely and inaccurately in recent times, leading to much confusion about how exactly to make use of the practice. Certain people use the term "meditate" to refer to contemplating or thinking about something, while others think of it as a state of fantasizing or daydreaming. But the meditation that we're going to refer to in this book is something else entirely.

<u>Meditation Explained</u>

Meditation is a method that allows the mind to rest and get into a state of mind that is entirely different from the ordinary mental space we usually operate from. It's a way to fathom ourselves on a deeper level and experience consciousness in a direct way. Meditation doesn't belong to any specific religion. Instead, it's a process that has verified results, defined principles, and works in a specific way. Meditation makes your mind:

- **Focused inwardly:** Meditation slows down your thought processes, allowing you to see them for what they are. However, this doesn't come until you've been practicing it for a while. At first, the stream of thoughts you witness in your own mind can seem quite chaotic, which is totally normal for beginners.

- **Relaxed:** In a state of meditation, your muscles can finally unclench, and your mind can take a break. It brings a very satisfying sense of much-needed relaxation to the participant, allowing them to reflect in a deeper way than usual.

- **Clear and calm:** Our minds tend to be very busy and clouded on an average day. Mediation is a way to clear it out and gain insights that you may not have had access to before. Meditation is not a sleepy state (unless perhaps you were already very tired before you began) but is instead a state of alert awareness.

Eventually, meditation leads to a silent mental space where deep contemplation can happen. It requires patience and a commitment to stick to the practice. All of the work you put into meditation will pay off in the end. If you meditate, the wonderful benefits of the practice will be yours to gain. We will cover these in detail throughout this book.

There are many books out there on the topic of meditation, so thank you sincerely for choosing this one. Let's begin the first steps of your journey with meditation.

Chapter 1: The Benefits, Science, and History

The concept of meditation is simple in theory; just sit still, notice your breathing, and let your mind settle down. But anyone who has tried this already knows that it's not always so easy. The practice of meditation is an ancient pursuit that has a deep history.

The History of Meditation

Among the earliest of written records detailing meditation practice are from 1500 BCE in Hindu tradition. The Hindu Vedas mention the traditions existent in ancient India. By the 5th century BCE or so, the practice had developed in other forms in Buddhist India and Taoist China. It also had its place (and still does) in Sikhism, Jainism, Judaism, and more. As you can see, it is a very important foundational aspect for various religions. Some believe it brings them closer to God.

The spread of meditation on the Silk Road helped the practice to gain ground across Asia. Once the practice arrived somewhere new, it would change and shift to fit into the culture of each respective area. But it's quite recent that meditation reached beyond certain religions in the western world. Now, it's reached far beyond religious purposes.

The Science and Medical Benefits of Meditation

In a cover story reported by TIME magazine in 2003, the practice was studied seriously in the '60s for its medical benefits. A researcher found that certain yogis were able to meditate so deeply that they didn't react to extremely hot objects touching their skin while in the trance state.

- **Research on Meditation:** But even so, the practice remained on the edges of modern science as mainstream researchers brushed it off. Then, in 1967, a professor at Harvard discovered that people who meditated lowered their heart rates, used less oxygen, and got into a mental state that was conducive to sleep and relaxation.

- **Biological Processes:** The researcher then published material on his findings and pioneered for the benefits of meditation on human biology. The researcher stated that he's made it his work to give a biological explanation for methods that people have already been using for many centuries.

- **Celebrity Status:** Around that same era, meditation gained celebrity status which garnered more scientific attention for the topic. In 1975, a TIME story was published that described Transcendental Meditation as a "high" without the need for drugs. The Beatles used Transcendental Meditation to cope with their overwhelming global fame and even studied it in India. It became quite a trendy topic during the hippie eras.

Meditation in Modern Day

By the '90s, the celebrity and scientific information on meditation came to an understanding somewhere in the center. The result was a health-focused idea that no longer carried the hippie implications that shrouded it before. People also started realizing that meditation didn't necessarily have to be a religious activity. Deepak Chopra, the author, played a role in spreading the word with his writing and appearance on Oprah.

Even athletes started talking about mindfulness and meditation. And at the same time, the scientific studies continued coming in showing how many benefits it could bring to practitioners. Meditation can:

- Manage stress and anxiety

- Reduce pain in those who practice it

- Potentially slow down neurodegeneration

- Encourages healthier choices

- Increases happiness

- Helps you concentrate

- Strengthens the immune system

And that's not all. MRI scans have proven that after two months of meditation and mindfulness, the amygdala (the part of the brain responsible for our fight or flight response) seems to get smaller. This area of our brain is responsible for fear and stress. In other words, if you need help reducing anxiety, nervousness, or fear, meditation is the way to go! We will give you some more specific tips for handling these problems, along with insomnia, in chapter five. But first, let's go over common challenges of meditation and elements of the practice.

Chapter 2: Common Challenges and Elements of Meditation

As stated, meditation sure is simple in theory, but what about practicing it? It doesn't take the average person long to discover that meditation can be a bit tougher than it sounded at first. Let's look over some of the common reasons people find it challenging to meditate so you can overcome them:

Trouble Relaxing

This might seem familiar to you. You just got home from a stressful, long day, and just want to go to sleep. But as soon as you get in bed, you can't shut off your brain no matter how hard you try. In fact, trying to calm yourself down appears to make you even more anxious and stressed out than before. This also happens often when you try to sit down to meditate. No matter how much you want to focus on your breath, your brain continues to obsess about something else.

How can you solve this problem? It's hard to calm down when your mind is already in a frenzy, since it's already caught up in a story and can't focus on something else. To release yourself from this state of agitation, it's best to first focus on something external. Here are some examples:

- **Taking a Walk:** Before trying to sit down and meditate, you could free yourself of some nervous tension by taking a walk around the block. Take in the nature around you and allow it to absorb your worries so you can return to the cushion (or chair) with a clear head.

- **Talking to Someone:** Another option is to talk to a friend or relative about whatever is troubling you, or just have a casual chat. Call someone up or meet someone for a coffee if you're agitated, then do your meditation later.

- **Listening to Music:** Music can be a great tool for calming the mind to get you prepared for a meditative state. Try listening to a few of your favorite songs to take your mind off your worries so you can relax, then return to your meditation practice.

<u>An Overactive Mind</u>

Another common issue is a wandering mind as you attempt to get into a meditative state. This could look like a thousand random thoughts appearing in your head as soon as you try to concentrate, or loud self-talk that won't be quiet. If this happens to you, you can follow these instructions:

- **Count Your Breaths:** Counting your breaths is one effective way to make your mind calm down. Basically, you just inhale as you normally would, then exhale, and count that as "one." Keep going.

- **Count to 10:** Go up to 10 breath cycles before you start over again. Keep in mind that you will probably get distracted many times when you're doing this, especially as a beginner, but that it does get easier over time.

- **Other Ideas:** Keep it interesting by mixing it up. You can count to 100, count backward, or count to an odd number like seven. The important thing is not the way you choose to do this, but that you're keeping your mind focused on something.

Not Having Enough Time

Another common issue is having a schedule that is so full that meditation seems like an impossible task to fit in. Or perhaps an important task always seems to pop up right as you are about to do your meditation session, making the practice inconsistent and sporadic, limiting its advantages. You can solve that by following these steps:

- **Wake Up Earlier:** One way to fit meditation into your day is to simply set your alarm for 15 minutes earlier than you normally would. This might be a struggle at first, but you will soon adjust to it.

- **Squeeze It in:** Another option is simply squeezing meditation in wherever you can fit it, whether this is in your car before driving to work, or on your break at school. Any meditation is better than none at all!

- **Clear your Schedule:** Now this one may seem a bit drastic, but I guess it depends how dedicated you are to gaining the benefits of this practice. Clear out some time in your schedule to make time for meditation, such as the time you spend on Facebook.

Falling Asleep when You Meditate

Drowsiness often happens to beginner meditators.
You may even mistake your drowsiness or nodding off
for a true meditation because you're feeling very
comfortable, calm, and your mind is actually quiet.
But spacing out or nodding off during meditation just
means that you have slid into dullness and aren't
awake and aware as you should be during meditation.
This gets you stuck in a mental fog that doesn't allow
you to see clearer, which is the goal of the practice,
after all.

If your main goal with meditating is to be more
relaxed, then this isn't necessarily a negative thing.
But if you want to advance spiritually, gain insights, or
become more focused and clear-minded you have to
overcome this dull drowsiness when you meditate. So,
how can you combat this? There are a number of
ways:

- **Check Your Posture:** Next time you feel yourself getting sleepy as you meditate, make sure that your posture is erect and straight. If it's not, consciously straighten your spine, lift your head, and take a deep breath to get more energy. Don't allow yourself to lean up against anything as this can encourage the muscles to relax a bit too much, leading to sleepiness or drowsiness. This is especially true if you're already tired.

- **Get Up:** If you're still feeling sleepy, you may need to get up and do a few jumping jacks or get some water. You could also try splashing water onto your face which is a great way to wake yourself up. Then you can return to your practice with a clearer mind.

- **Don't Meditate after Eating:** Another good guideline for reducing drowsiness during your practice is avoiding meditation right after you eat, as this can make you feel sleepy already. Try to do it on an empty stomach or at least an hour after meals, instead.

<u>Visions, Lights, or Colors</u>

Certain beginner meditators will see a lot of colors or visions behind their eyelids, which is distracting or disturbing to them. Other new meditators might be bothered by the fact that they don't see anything when they shut their eyes. To start with, seeing visions or lights isn't proof of advancement in meditation. Many meditation masters exist who are spiritually advanced, wise, super focused, and don't see any visions when they close their eyes. Here are some tips to deal with these expectations:

- **Don't Expect Anything:** Start by not having any specific hopes or expectations for your meditation sessions. Instead, learn the art of becoming so focused on a single thing that nothing else exists at that moment.

- **Don't get Distracted:** And if you do see anything behind your eyelids when you meditate, try not to focus on it too much or get too excited as this can just be a distraction from your concentration. Stay calm and allow it to be there.

Distracting Body Sensations

Some people might feel distracting sensations during their meditation, like warmth, cold, tingling or even cramps. How can you handle this to minimize the distraction and keep your focus where it belongs?

- **Fix the Environment:** Are you in an environment that is too hot or cold? Maybe you have your ankles crossed which is causing your foot to go numb and tingle, or maybe you're clasping your hands too tightly.

- **Choose the Right Position:** If you aren't comfortable while you meditate, it's a sign that you need to change to a better position. You could be trying to sit up too straight to where it's causing pain or pressure, or sitting cross-legged without the flexibility it requires. Try out a few different postures until you find what works.

- **Stretching:** One great way to help minimize discomfort during your meditation sessions is doing some stretching before you sit down. This will help improve your circulation and prevent annoying tingling sensations. Doing this will help you better focus on your meditation when you do it.

The Elements of Meditation Practice

From our time as children, we've been taught to verify and examine things in the world outside of us. Most of us were not told how to verify truths, find answers, or look within ourselves. This makes us strangers to our own inner beings as we focus on the external world. This disconnection from our truer nature is one contributing factor to confusion and unhealthy relationships, among other common problems.

Gaining Clarity:

The part of our minds that most of us focus on, listen to constantly, and live from on a day to day basis, is only a tiny part of who we are. The piece of us that sleeps and dreams, and our deep, vast subconscious mind, remains undisciplined and mysterious to us. This is outside of our control, and we are taught to accept this. But the subconscious mind doesn't have to be a mystery to us. We can get to know it. Meditation is one way to get to know this deeper part of ourselves and start aligning with who we truly want to be.

Going Beyond

The point of meditation is going beyond our experiences and seeing deeper into our truer nature, which is blissful, happy, and peaceful. But most people who attempt to meditate already know that the mind is often frantic and stands in the way of being aware on a deeper level. Our minds are unruly and undisciplined, and it fights against our best attempts to make it behave. It seems to be its own entity, at times. This explains why some people sit down to meditate and only have daydreams or fantasies the whole time. They can't seem to reach the still, calm place of genuine meditation.

Teaching Ourselves Stillness

Most of us are told how to behave and move in the world, but not how to pay attention to ourselves and be calm and still. When we teach ourselves this by meditating, the highest joys of life can be ours for the taking. All joys of life pass by quickly, but meditation brings something far greater. Many sages have renounced their worldly possessions for this reason. This is not to say that you should do this, by any means. Only meant to show the power of this practice.

Seeing the Truth

Meditation is the most practical way to calm yourself, see the world for what it is, and release your biases and prejudices. It's a method for making your mind more disciplined, so you don't have to be caught up in the endless chaos. Yes, it's true, you can become free of this! Meditation is a way of exploring the universe that exists inside you. It's a serious commitment you must take on; the goal of getting to know the true you, your path, and the nature of reality. Being calm doesn't have to be something religious, but should be learned for the sake of health and sanity.

The Cultivation of Stillness

Figuring out how to be calm and still is the purpose of a meditation practice. This process starts inside of you. In yoga, students are guided by a teacher to sit up straight in a posture of meditation. As soon as they have figured out how to feel comfortable sitting that way, they practice in that position, in the same place, and at the same time each day. We will cover the first steps now on how to meditate, with other methods outlined throughout the book:

1. Choose a Place

Find a quiet, uncluttered, and simple place that will remain undisturbed for the duration of this practice. Then sit down on a chair or cushion, keeping your eyes shut and your back erect.

2. Moving Awareness

Next, you're going to move your awareness throughout the body, letting your muscles get relaxed as you go. Allow yourself to enjoy the feeling of releasing tension in all of your muscles. Meditation is about letting go, and you can start this in your body first.

3. Belly Breathing

As soon as you feel relaxed and peaceful, become aware of your breathing. Pay attention to where this breathing is taking place. If you are primarily breathing through your chest, you'll have a hard time completely relaxing. Instead, breathe through your belly, allowing it to expand as you go. You will get used to this over time.

4. Refrain from Judgment

Now, this is perhaps the hardest part of the whole process. Meditation is about letting go of all judgments about yourself, others, or the situation. Focus your attention on your breathing and let it happen with full acceptance. Don't judge what's happening or try to control it too much.

5. Let the Thoughts Pass

You are going to notice countless thoughts popping up as you attempt to focus on your breath. You may be wondering how much longer you are going to be doing this for, whether or not you're doing it "right," or whether you need to make a call right at that moment. Allow them to pass by without attaching any judgment to them. This will be difficult at first but get easier with time.

Now, you might start to notice that the thoughts become less frantic when you let them pass by instead of reacting to them. You may even start to see the true nature of your mind, which is often pure chaos. The mind is not the problem; the problem is when you allow the content of the mind to stir you up and disturb you deeply. But if you can make a practice of just letting the thoughts be, noticing them, and letting them pass with no reaction, you are doing as well as you possibly can. This is how you learn to control your own mental reactions.

A Vacation in Yourself

Meditation is essentially allowing yourself to take a relaxing vacation without having to leave your house. It's a very simple process of attending. Start with attending to (noticing) the breath, and when your thoughts come, let them be there and pass by, returning again to your breathing. You do this over and over again, as many times as it takes until it's an ingrained habit.

The normal reaction is to pay attention to each thought that passes by and this is why so many humans are frantic and discontent in their lives, living in a confused state. Meditation allows you to let your thoughts be with no reaction. This teaches you that you are much more than just your mind.

Freedom from Your Mind

This process brings you eventual freedom from the meandering of the mind, allowing you to see who you are apart from this confused turmoil inside your head. You will feel contentment and joy, inner relaxation and true relief. This is the vacation within yourself. Then you can apply these lessons to your activities as you go about your life. Meditation isn't meant to be an escape from reality, but a tool that helps you handle it in a better way.

Reactions to Life

Normally, people respond to their outer experiences in a very similar way to how they respond to the thoughts they have. If you hear an angry remark from someone, it may lead you to become depressed or upset. If you can't find something important, you get anxious or sad. The events in your life are what control your inner state; not you. This makes life a very chaotic rollercoaster ride. We may even feel like we don't have a say in our own reactions as they often happen so fast that they feel like something separate from us.

You might interpret the things you hear or see based on your own resistances, prejudices, fears, or expectations instead of seeing reality for what it is. This leads you to block off the experience and limit yourself to a small world of choices instead of remaining creative, open and aware in your life. If, on the other hand, you learn how to use the principles you learn in your meditation practice, you can be present for the events in your life. You can control your own responses.

Noticing and Choosing

Meditation allows you to notice your initial kneejerk reaction and choose whether or not you will respond in that way. You can pay attention and see when you feel threatened or angry instead of flying off the handle immediately and then having to pick up the pieces later. Stay open to your experiences, allowing them to pass by instead of getting stuck in them. Then you can constructively choose the emotions that will help you build a better life.

Giving Yourself Therapy

Meditation is a therapeutic practice that you can give yourself. This gift brings you stability, balance, and sheds light on the most confusing of inner processes. You will see the unproductive parts of yourself, your immaturities, and your problems. These are all things that we find difficult to look at, but meditation helps with this. As you focus your attention on these negative aspects, they diminish.

Consistency

At first, meditation will likely feel like a difficult chore to you, as any new practice does. Eventually, however, you will start to look forward to it when you see how much joy and clarity it can bring to who you are. Consistency is key in this area. Give yourself the gift of your own awareness with a faithful practice of

meditation.

Chapter 3: Preparation, Practice, and Habit

Meditation is a well-known and studied practice that can reduce pain, depression, and anxiety symptoms. Evidence has also suggested that those experienced with meditation experienced changes at molecular and genetic levels, leading to lower inflammation. But regardless of these amazing advantages, many beginner meditators give up as soon as they hit an obstacle along the way. This is understandable because a lot of them believe meditation is simple and therefore easy. After all, sitting down and "doing nothing" can't be that hard, right?

But meditation is not doing nothing, and it's anything but a passive activity. At its core, meditation is actively changing and training your mind to be more resilient, focused, and mindful. Our culture is obsessed with instant results, making these traits in very short supply. Meditation training will require commitment and serious effort. You will also need to dedicate time to it to bring about real, lasting, beneficial changes.

Proper Preparation for Your Practice

A lot of beginners don't realize that dealing with complications is just part of the process. If you can overcome obstacles along the way, it just solidifies and strengthens the practice, making you even stronger. And there are countless solutions for making meditation easier. It all starts with proper preparation. Most of us are busy, so efficiency is key to practices of any kind.

Quality over Quantity

When it comes to meditation, quality is more important than quantity. Only 15 minutes of calm, focused meditation will have more benefit than a forced hour of distracted meditation full of daydreaming. Here are some other tips that will help you get in the zone for your meditation.

Get the Space Ready

Simple actions like lighting some incense or candles, making sure your phone is either off or in a different room or choosing a room that you feel comfortable in can all make a huge difference in your practice. Consider this as your "warmup" for the practice. Just like with jogging, you have to prepare yourself to meditate, so your session goes well. Not doing this might make it harder to concentrate or quiet your mind.

Know Your Intentions

Choosing an intention as you prepare for your meditation can help you get more value out of the experience. This will help set a direction to keep your focus on. Any time you choose to do this before your practice, you are getting into alignment with the overall purpose and won't get distracted as easily. If you're having a hard time figuring out what your intention is, simply ask yourself why you chose this practice. It might be a spiritual reason, having a chance to relax, or improving your focus for your studies. Connecting with the intention is going to give you the support you need to stay dedicated.

Be Curious

Similar to setting your meditation intention, coming up with a question to ask before meditation is a powerful, simple method for getting the most out of it.

Go with questions that are open such as "What am I?" or "What is reality?" If you can't figure out a good question to ask, spend some time thinking about it before you proceed. You may also find it helpful to write about it, which brings us to the next tip.

Record Your Distractions

Eventually, you'll have a day where you can't stop wondering when your friend is going to call or what you forget to add to your grocery list while you're sitting down to meditate. One way to combat these distractions is to write down any thoughts that are bouncing around in your head before you sit down. You might also keep a pen and paper near you so you can record anything that pops up that you're afraid of forgetting. Getting your thoughts out on paper like this will free up your mental space, making more room for focused awareness and a meditative state.

Try Binaural Beats

If these tips still don't allow you to calm down enough to meditate, you can try listening to some binaural beats. These will focus your mind and allow you to calm down as they help bring your brain into relaxed states. Simply search for "binaural beats" on YouTube and enjoy!

<u>Sticking with the Meditation Habit</u>

As with any other habit, the hardest part of meditation is making yourself do it every day no matter what. If you're dedicated to sticking with this new habit each and every day, follow these tips.

1. Be Realistic

You may think it's a noble goal to set an hour per day for your meditation practice, but this makes it less likely that you'll stick with your new habit. Instead, try choosing a realistic and easily achievable amount of time, such as 15 minutes. There may be some days where you only have time to do 10 or feel like going beyond 15 to do 20 minutes. However, setting a realistic minimum will give you a sense of achievement any time you meet the goal and keep you on your path.

2. Meditate Anywhere

Physical exercise can only be done at certain times because it involves the hassle of needing specific clothes, usually needing a shower afterward, and more. But meditation has the benefit of being purely mental, meaning it can be done anytime and anywhere. Look for opportunities throughout the day to sneak some more meditation practice in. Here are some ideas for times and places to do it:

- While standing in line at the grocery store

- In the elevator

- While you're on the bus

- At the park

- At your desk at work

When you're new to your practice, you'll probably need a quiet environment to do your meditation, but one of the benefits of getting used to the practice is that you can start doing it anywhere. Noise eventually won't bother you as much anymore.

3. Meditate Early in the Day

The next tip is meditating in the morning instead of later on in the day. Most people are in a calmer frame of mind when they first wake up and meditating can add an extra level of peace to bring with you as you go about your busy schedule. If this doesn't work, choose another time and try to make it the same, such as a quick meditation session on your break at work. You don't have to adhere to this precisely every time, but having a general time of day set aside for meditation will further ingrain the habit for you.

4. Don't Break the Chain

Get a calendar where you can mark off each day that you stick with your meditation practice. You can even try counting how many days in a row you do. It will be much harder to break a streak of say, 35 days than it will to just rationalize skipping your practice when you haven't been keeping track. The calendar method has the benefit of showing you a physical representation of your newfound habit and makes you not want to break your streak. Every time you make it an entire week without skipping your practice, make sure you find a way to give yourself a small reward!

5. Be Flexible

A solid meditation practice requires that the one practicing it is flexible. Life can be unpredictable, and this is worth remembering. Even though you're dedicated to the path, there will be some days where you don't have time to complete as long of a session as you would have hoped. Perhaps you'll get sick, have to travel for work, or just won't have enough energy to sit in a meditative position for 20 minutes. On days like these, try to fit in some mini-meditations throughout the day. Even doing short sessions like this is better than nothing and there's no point in beating yourself up because you can't do the full amount of time you wanted to do.

6. Accept Imperfection

Most of us have very critical brains. We suffer from thoughts such as "I should just give up" or "I'm no good at this." But it's thoughts like these that can be helped by sticking with meditation. Meditation is training your mind, and when you're practicing something, it's fine to not be perfect at it. You may think that each time you notice your mind wandering, it's a sign of failure, but exactly the opposite is true. Noticing your distractions is the entire purpose of this practice, so see it as a good thing. If you aren't noticing it when your mind strays, you're not really meditating.

7. See it as an Altruistic Activity

People who don't meditate might have the wrong idea about it, assuming it's an inherently selfish activity that doesn't help others at all. But the fact is that when you learn how to be more comfortable with yourself, you are a better person who treats others with more respect. Developing your meditation skills also improves your empathy, patience, and acceptance of others. When you can't seem to motivate yourself to sit down to meditate for the reasons you normally

think about, imagine the people in your life you'll be
helping by doing so.

8. It's not a Miracle Cure

Meditation is great, as we've been saying in this book,
but it isn't a miracle cure for all of your problems.
Even when you are a seasoned meditator, you'll still
feel sadness, stress, and anxiety because those
emotions are part of being human. You might have an
urge to think your practice isn't yielding any results
when you have these moods, but remember that
noticing them is a step in the right direction! It means
your practice is paying off. Normally, people have a
negative mood and don't notice it, allowing it to run
unchecked and even ruin their day.

The fact is that stress is just a part of existing. Meditation won't eradicate this entirely, but it will give you the tools necessary to see these emotions come up and choose a more constructive way to handle them. Instead of looking back at events in your life and wondering what came over you and made you act in such foolish ways, you'll be able to slow down your mind and choose healthy responses. This will give you better relationships and more patience at work. You don't have to let your feelings run you. You are in control!

9. Don't Compare Yourself to Others

This is a habit that nearly everyone on earth is guilty of partaking in at some point or another. We look to those who we think are better than us at certain activities and compare ourselves. But this is just an excuse to beat yourself up. Don't look at people who you believe are "better" than you at meditation. Instead, focus on yourself and improve however you can. This is how you will truly advance with your practice.

10.   Enjoy Your Practice

Even though a disciplined approach is necessary for sticking with meditation, that doesn't mean you can't enjoy what you're doing. It isn't something you only practice for a short while until you're cured and then stop doing. It's something you stick with throughout life and continue to improve at. Instead of only engaging in meditation for the benefits it will bring you, try to remember to enjoy the path to getting there, as well. Remember that it's a method for giving yourself a free vacation and that it can be a nice

activity in and of itself.

Chapter 4: Alternative Methods for Meditation

Thousands of individuals have started meditating to bring more personal health into their lives. To become as healthy as possible, it's crucial to exercise as often as you can, eat healthy foods, and take care of your mental health. People have a hard time improving their mental well-being. It's not that we don't have the ability, but that most of us haven't been taught how to do it, and don't see tangible results from the effort we put in. Meditation is one way of reducing stress and becoming more tranquil and peaceful in life.

Meditation Techniques to Try

In this chapter, we will go over some different styles of meditation so you can choose the one that appeals most to you. Don't be afraid to experiment with each type or even mix and match as you go about your practice. Remember, it should be something enjoyable, not a chore!

Heart Rhythm Meditation

This is a meditation where the focus is primarily placed on the heart and breathing. Doing this can help you feel more connected to the world around you and experience spiritual and mental connection. It will also connect you with joy and reduce stress. If you're unsure of how to do this, keep practicing, and it will get easier.

Transcendental Meditation

Also called TM, this method of meditation helps you get on the path towards enlightenment, bring a quiet state of mind and calmness. This tradition is Hindu in origin and involves sitting cross-legged, chanting

mantras, and focusing on positivity. You can find

resources for learning this meditation online, but they

may involve a fee. If you don't want to pay for your

meditation resource, search for another type.

Kundalini Meditation

This is a meditation style that aims to focus the energy

in your body, allowing it to rise up. This type of

practice has been used in both Hindu and Buddhist

traditions. A lot of people see this meditation style as

a metaphorical action of uncoiling the energy at the

base of your spine. But other people take it quite

literally and believe it has amazing healing powers. To

gain access to this energy, the person practicing

Kundalini meditation has to concentrate their focus

and breath through the different centers of energy in

the body. This brings about a state of altered consciousness.

Zazen Meditation

This is at the center of Zen Buddhism and means "seated meditation." This practice is easier than others to engage in at first because it's self-guided. But some practitioners may find that not having a guide makes it harder. It really depends on your personality. Zazen aims to help you forget about distracting images, judgmental ideas, and negative thoughts. To do this, just sit as straight as possible and follow the breath into a state of awareness. Continue to bring your attention back to the breath any time it strays.

Guided Meditations

Guided meditations can help for people who are new to this and have a really hard time slowing their minds down. It can be beneficial for personal development, relieving stress, and healing the spiritual world. You can find guided meditations on YouTube. If you're a visual learner, try to find a guided visualization that will talk you through mental images you can explore during your meditation practice.

Qi Gong

This meditation style can improve relaxation, respiration, and posture in those who practice it. It's an old method that comes from the ancient society in China. This style of wellness and health uses the breath to bring your energy through your energy centers in the body. Focusing on movement, breathing techniques, and relaxation, this style allows those who practice it to have more control over how they respond to stressful stimuli in their lives.

Mindfulness Meditation

Another calming and effective method of meditation is basic mindfulness, also originating in Buddhist traditions. Bringing about mindfulness in your mental state is crucial for overcoming difficulties in life and gaining access to your natural wisdom. It allows you to acknowledge the true nature of reality by accepting your thoughts as they come up instead of resisting them. Sounds simple, right? But it can be a challenge in practice. To do mindfulness meditation, simply sit down with a straight back, either in a chair or on a cushion in the middle of the floor. Focus on your breathing and allow your thoughts to come up, watching them carefully. Studies have proven that this type of meditation helps reduce stress, anxiety, and depression symptoms.

Finding Your Style

You will naturally like certain styles of meditation more than others. Not all of them will be the best for you. Try each one on our list to see what is best for achieving the state of mental calm you're aiming for. As soon as you've found a method that clicks with you, stick with it every single day. Being faithful to your practice is far more important than the type of meditation you choose to practice.

Chapter 5: Tricks for Relieving Anxiety, Depression, and Insomnia

Most people feel unsure and stuck when they get anxious, not knowing what to do to turn their mood around. You may even unintentionally make your anxiety even stronger by obsessing about the future or ruminating about something that happened earlier in the day. You may ask yourself what could go wrong and run through endless scenarios, making yourself more upset with each passing thought. And worst of all, you may even bash yourself and judge your own thoughts and anxiety, believing in all the worst-case ideas you can come up with.

How to Reduce Anxiety

But it doesn't have to be this way. You can change these patterns. There are many different techniques and tools you can implement to help curb your anxiety. Meditation is, of course, a great place to start, but there are other tricks you can use to make it even more effective. Let's look a little closer at these now.

Deep Breathing

The best thing to do as soon as you start feeling anxious is to take a deep breath. There's a reason why this advice is so cliché and well-known; because it works! Deep breathing from the belly can reduce your anxiety because it automatically turns on the relaxation response in your body, soothing your nervous feelings. Inhale for four seconds, filling up your belly and chest, hold the breath for four seconds, and then exhale for four seconds. Repeat this until you feel better.

Acceptance

The next crucial step is accepting where you are with your anxious thoughts. Anxiety is nothing but an emotion, just like any other. When you remind yourself that it's just a feeling reaction instead of an emergency, acceptance becomes much easier. Acceptance is a must because attempting to force yourself to stop feeling anxious just makes it worse, as you likely already know. It only feeds the false notion that anxiety is unacceptable or intolerable.

Contrary to what you may think, when you accept anxious feelings, you aren't giving up or accepting misery. Instead, you're being realistic and allowing yourself to let your emotions flow through and pass. All emotions will naturally pass on their own if you don't resist them. So next time, try acceptance!

See the Illusion

When you're in a panicked frenzy of anxious thoughts, your brain is messing with you. Realizing this can help you combat anxiety. A panic attack can actually feel like a severe health issue, but it isn't. You will not die from anxiety, even if it feels like you might at any moment, and it pays to remind yourself of this.

Question Reality

Anytime someone gets anxious, their minds begin throwing outlandish ideas at them. No matter how unlikely or unrealistic these ideas are, the anxious mind will latch onto them and feed them with fear. Next time these thoughts start to run through your head, try questioning them instead. Say you're about to give a presentation at work and immediately think, "I cannot do this, I'm going to fail and embarrass myself." Instead of instantly believing the thought and letting it grow in intensity, remind yourself that the situation isn't an emergency and that you've survived fear before.

But when we're anxious, we often perceive events as worse than they really are. Even if you do mess up on your presentation, the people in the audience will be so concerned with their own thoughts that they will probably hardly notice. Here are some questions you can ask yourself next time you feel anxious:

- Am I being realistic right now?

- What is the likeliest outcome of this event?

- Can I handle it if things go wrong?

- What can I do to help this situation?

- Is there a way to prepare that I haven't thought of yet?

- Am I getting carried away with fear right now?

Learn How to Visualize

Practice this meditation on a regular basis, and it will help you gain access to peace next time you're feeling nervous. Imagine that you're next to a lake or river at your favorite place. Feel the sun on your face, hear the water, and sense your calm state of mind. Imagine that each cloud floating by is one of your emotions, and allow them to pass. Emotions are not inherently good or bad. They are neutral, and we assign labels to them. But you don't have to do this. Remember that

every feeling is neutral and that you can choose how
to handle it.

Observe with No Judgment

One of the main goals of your meditation can be
observing your judgment, sensations, feelings, and
thoughts with a compassionate attitude instead of the
judgment you would usually have. Write this goal
down and keep it somewhere highly visible so you can
be reminded of what it says.

Using Positive Words

Most of us aren't very mindful of how we speak to
ourselves, and that just makes anxiety worse. Instead
of allowing yourself to engage in hateful, self-
destructive talk in your head, focus instead on positive

words. Remind yourself that you are strong, capable, and worthy of love.

Be Present-focused

Anxiety can only exist when you are projecting yourself into the past or future. When you're present in the hear and now, it goes away. Next time you're obsessing about something that already happened or will happen, remember that you can't control anything other than your attitude in the present moment. Take some deep breaths, do a short meditation, and return to the situation with new eyes.

Stay Busy

Any time you're feeling anxious, it can be hard to accomplish the tasks that you normally would throughout the day, but this is exactly what you should do. Instead of sitting down and obsessing, avoiding your tasks, or distracting yourself, go about your to-do list as if it were just an ordinary day. Be busy, and your anxious feelings will fade naturally as all emotions do.

Tricks for Relieving Depression

Depression is a difficult matter to deal with, but a few of these tips can help you manage it better. Although meditation can help with depression, don't neglect seeing a mental health professional if you feel it isn't enough. Here are the tips:

1. **Be Smart about Your Goals**

Choose some straightforward, easy goals that you can follow without much issue. They should be measurable, specific, rewarding, and possible. In other words, choosing that you will lose 20 pounds within a week isn't a realistic goal, but choosing to go for a walk each day is.

2. Avoid Dramatic Thinking

Thinking in black and white terms feeds depression. People who are feeling depressed tend to think that no one likes them or that they'll never amount to anything. This type of dramatic thinking just makes depression worse. Meditation can help a lot with separating yourself from these thoughts, but you can also try thinking in gray shades instead of black and white. Instead of using language such as "always" or "never," ask yourself how realistic you're being and find a statement that more accurately reflects reality. For example, if you think "I'll never get a job," immediately replace it with, "I will find a job because I have done so many times in the past."

Fake It till you Make It

When you're depressed, you will probably stop doing the activities that you care about most in the world. Make a list of these activities, such as taking walks, seeing friends, or cooking at home. Even if you don't feel like it, start reintroducing each of these activities into your schedule. Odds are, once you begin following through with them, some of your enthusiasm will return, and you'll feel better. Even taking care of errands can make you feel better than sitting around and doing nothing.

Look for Evidence

Depressive thoughts are rarely realistic. Next time you feel depressed, remember that your thoughts are likely colored by the mental state and aren't based on evidence. As soon as a negative thought comes up, ask to see the evidence of it. Odds are, you won't find any evidence for the belief that "Everyone hates me." Decide to stop repeating these harmful ideas to yourself, and never assume you know what others think of you unless you've asked.

Accept the Mental State

The worst thing you can do when you feel depressed is deny it. If your situation sucks at the moment, just accept where you are. That's the only way you can move past it. Acceptance is the only way to relieve

your state of suffering because it opens up your mind
to see solutions.

Be Nice to Yourself

Treating yourself with respect is another important
foundation for a healthy mentality in life. Pay
attention to how you speak to yourself compared to
how you talk to other people. If you're way meaner to
yourself than you are to others (which you likely are in
this case), make an effort to be gentler and kinder in
your self-talk. Think about whether you'd use the
same words you talk to yourself with while comforting
your best friend. If not, the language has no place in
your mind.

Find Structure

Even when you aren't in the mood, always follow a schedule of some kind. Set your alarm for the morning, eat lunch at the same time, and go to sleep around the same time, as well. When you're depressed, it's easy to fall into habits of sleeping or eating inconsistently. Even when you're feeling down or are unemployed, setting a structured routine is important as it can give you a reliable setting to focus on. Bonus points if you can fit socializing into the routine.

Tricks to Relieve Sleeplessness

What is insomnia? It's being unable to either fall or stay asleep, which results in non-restorative and unrefreshing rest at night. Everyone needs different amounts of rest at night, so insomnia can be defined as how you feel after waking up instead of how fast you can fall asleep or the amount of hours you stay asleep. Even for those who lie down for eight hours every night, waking up feeling fatigued and drowsy could still mean they have insomnia.

When it comes to sleep complaints, insomnia is the most common, but it doesn't refer to just one sleep disorder. It makes more sense to call it a symptom of a problem than the problem itself. Whatever issue is causing sleeplessness will be different between individuals. It could be that you have a medical condition or that you've simply had too much coffee that day.

Symptoms of Insomnia

Thankfully, most insomnia can be fixed by making personal changes without sleeping pills or visiting a professional. Let's look at some common symptoms of insomnia:

- Being tired but still having trouble falling asleep

- Waking up a lot throughout the night

- Not being able to fall asleep again after waking up

- Waking up in the morning still very tired

- Needing alcohol or drugs to get to sleep at night

- Waking up earlier than you want to repeatedly

- Being irritable, tired, or drowsy during the day

- Having a hard time concentrating due to tiredness

Potential Causes

To be able to cure or treat your sleeplessness, you have to start paying attention. This is where meditation can be a great help. Emotional problems like depression or anxiety are the cause of at least 50 percent of cases of insomnia. But the habits you have during the day and before sleeping can also play a part in sleeplessness. In addition, your physical habits play a role. Try to indicate all potential causes of sleeplessness, and as soon as you've found a root issue, you can work on treating it. Here are some potential causes of insomnia:

- Are you going through something stressful in your life?

- Do you feel hopeless, flat, or depressed?

- Have you experienced trauma recently?

- Are you suffering from constant worry or anxiety?

- Did you recently start any new medications?

- Is there a health issue that might be causing the issue?

- Is your bedroom comfortable and quiet for sleeping?

- Do you have a consistent schedule of sleeping and waking?

Medical or Psychological Causes

At times, sleeplessness will only last a couple days and then goes away. This is especially true when it's from a temporary cause like jet lag, a breakup, or a presentation that's making you feel nervous. But other times, it sticks around. This is when it could be related to a physical or mental issue that you have yet to identify. Let's look at a list of medical or psychological causes for insomnia, some of which may require treatment from a professional:

- Anxiety disorder or recurring stress

- Depression or consistent sadness

- Persistent anger and frustration

- Trauma, grief, or bipolar disorder

- Asthma or allergies

- Acid reflux from diet problems

- Kidney issues

- Chronic pain

- Parkinson's disease

Sleep Disorders

Persistent insomnia is a sleep disorder itself, but may also signify a different sleep disorder like restless legs syndrome, sleep apnea, or disturbances in your circadian rhythm due to odd work hours or traveling.

Medications

Certain medications can cause sleeplessness, like some contraceptives, blood pressure meds, thyroid hormones, ADHD stimulants, and antidepressant medications. Flue and cold meditations might cause sleeplessness if they have alcohol in them. Diuretics, Model, Excedrin, and diet pills can also cause insomnia as they often have caffeine or other stimulants in them.

How to Figure Out the Cause

Although treating mental and underlying physical issues is good to start with, it won't always take away your insomnia completely. You should also take a look at the habits you engage in during the day as your coping methods for sleeplessness may actually contribute to the problem, in some cases. For instance, you might be relying on alcohol or sleeping pills to go to sleep at night, which only contributes to the issue over time. Or you might be drinking too much coffee at work, keeping you up at night. Here are some other habits that could contribute:

- Taking naps during the day

- Having too much sugar during the day

- Eating too much at night

- Exercising late in the day

- Not moving around enough

- Using your phone before bed

- Watching movies before sleep

These habits not only make insomnia worse but sleeping badly can make you rely on these habits even more, creating an unhealthy cycle. The only way to break out of this cycle is to change the habits contributing to it. At times, these simple changes will be enough to get rid of the insomnia issue. Give yourself a few days to get accustomed to this change, but as soon as you do, it could solve the problem.

Don't forget to look at habits that you may not typically associate with sleep problems. Some habits might be so automatic that you don't realize they can be a factor. You might have to give up your nightly glass of wine or phone habit before bed.

Keep a Sleep Journal

One reliable way to discover what could be causing your sleeplessness is keeping a dream journal. In this, you can record every noteworthy action you took during the day, such as having coffee or not having coffee. You can also write down the time you go to sleep and the time you wake up, the activities you engage in right before bed, how much exercise you got that day, mental stress factors, and more. Once you understand the contributing factors, you're ready to start...

Creating a Better Routine

You can get rid of insomnia with the right routine and sleep environment. The best weapons against this problem are a relaxing routine at night and a comfortable, quiet room to sleep in. These factors will make a huge difference. Observe the following tips, starting now:

- **Make your Room Cool and Dark:** Light, noise, and a warm room can all make it harder to sleep. In addition, make sure your pillow is the right one for you as the wrong shape can really disturb sleep patterns. If outside noise is keeping you up, try some earplugs or a fan to get rid of the sound. Dark curtains can help with the light as can a sleep mask. Try out different types of mattresses, if possible, as this can also contribute to sleep issues.

- **Make a No-screen Rule:** Before bed, you should have a rule that there are no electronic screens allowed near you. The blue light emitted by these devices contributes to sleep problems as it can disrupt melatonin production in the body. Get rid of your phone habit before bed and instead choose to listen to some music or read a book. Better yet, spend that extra time journaling or talking to your partner.

- **Be Consistent:** Stick with a consistent sleep schedule to support your internal clock. Do this even on the weekends, and you will be much likelier to fall into a reliable pattern of sleeping well. Wake up in the morning at the time you decided, even when you don't feel rested. This will encourage your circadian rhythm to get back on track and bring you restful nights.

- **Limit your Naps:** Naps can contribute to trouble sleeping at night. This doesn't mean you can't take naps; just that you should make sure they are short. Don't sleep for longer than 20 or 30 minutes if you're napping in the afternoon. Instead of taking a nap, try doing a meditation instead, and this will wake you up a bit and refresh you if you're feeling exhausted in the middle of the day.

- **No Stimulating Activities:** Before bedtime, don't allow yourself to engage in any stressful or stimulating activities like having huge

arguments, working, or checking your emails.
These can get the wheels in your head turning,
making it harder to calm your mind and rest
before sleep. This includes snacking on
stimulating or sugary foods, like chocolate.

- **Limit Liquids before Bed:** Another issue
  that causes insomnia is having to get up to use
  the bathroom. Try to limit your fluid intake
  before sleep, not having any water the last hour
  before lying down. This will help you get up
  less during the night. This includes alcohol
  since drinking disturbs your sleep patterns and
  makes you wake up more frequently in the
  night.

- **Large Meals:** Eating big meals too close to
  bedtime can keep you awake as your stomach

hasn't had time to digest the food. In addition, acidic or spicy foods might give you heartburn or stomach problems which make it harder to sleep. Limit eating at least two hours before lying down to go to sleep to get rid of this problem. And of course, don't have any caffeine in the afternoons or it could make you toss and turn at night. Switch instead to herbal tea with no caffeine after your morning cup of coffee.

The more you begin to have trouble sleeping, the easier it is to obsess and worry about it. You might even dread the nighttime because you're afraid you won't be able to sleep and will have to wake up exhausted. Or maybe you keep thinking that if you don't fall asleep *right now* you won't be rested and the day will be heard, which only makes it worse. But try your best not to dwell on these thoughts as they pump

up the adrenaline in your body and make you even
less tired. Be aware of every thought that crosses your
head and of course use the tools you've learned in
your meditation practice to help with sleeplessness.

Final Thoughts

Thank you for reading *Meditation for Beginners: How to Meditate and Find Tranquility, Relieve Stress and Anxiety, and Depression.* I hope you found it beneficial and are now inspired to start a lifelong relationship with meditation.

Noticing Benefits of Meditation

Please note that while some meditation benefits are apparent very quickly, others don't appear until quite a while after starting the practice. You may notice more calmness and physical relaxation very fast when you begin the practice, while later on, you might pick up on subtler changes in your life. Keep in mind that the most important benefits this practice brings will only come gradually and may not seem so dramatic.

Sticking to Your Practice

The hustles and bustles of everyday life, not to mention the alarming, changing environment we are in, cause us to worry about our life, our future, and security. Finding peace of mind is somehow difficult. But medication is a great help to fight anxiety. Stay true to meditation, and you'll notice that you eventually become free from worry. Then you can choose not to allow negative thoughts to take over your mind and ruin your day as they often do. You will then be free to live your life in the present moment. You will become a stronger, calmer, and all around better person for the effort you put in. In other words, it will be well worth your time!

As soon as you've gotten deeper into your meditation practice, you will be able to contribute to the world in a whole new way, sharing your newfound peace and joy and inspiring other people. If you found this book to be a helpful guide, please take the time to leave it a positive review on Amazon. Thank you and good luck

on your journey with meditation!

Furthermore, the transmission, duplication or reproduction of any of the following work, including precise information, will be considered an illegal act, irrespective whether it is done electronically or in print. The legality extends to creating a secondary or tertiary copy of the work or a recorded copy and is only allowed with an express written consent of the Publisher. All additional rights are reserved.

The information in the following pages is broadly considered to be a truthful and accurate account of facts, and as such any inattention, use or misuse of the information in question by the reader will render any resulting actions solely under their purview. There are no scenarios in which the publisher or the original author of this work can be in any fashion deemed liable for any hardship or damages that may befall them after undertaking information described herein.

Additionally, the information found on the following pages is intended for informational purposes only and should thus be considered, universal. As befitting its nature, the information presented is without assurance regarding its continued validity or interim quality. Trademarks that mentioned are done without written consent and can in no way be considered an endorsement from the trademark holder.